HOMEGROWN AND HANDPICKED

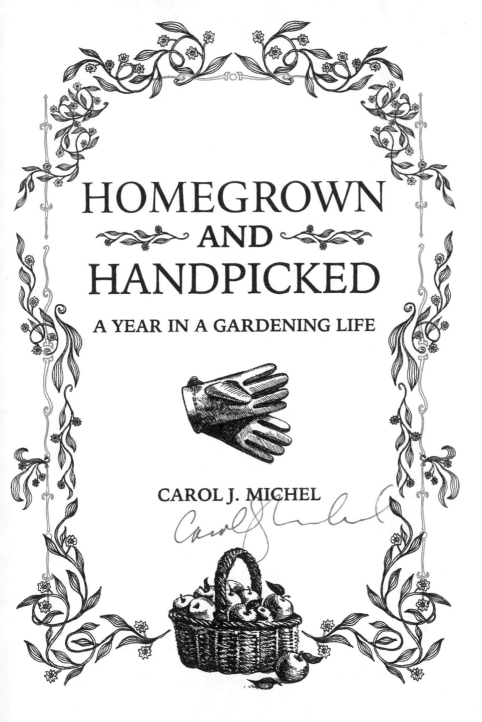

HOMEGROWN AND HANDPICKED

A YEAR IN A GARDENING LIFE

CAROL J. MICHEL

Gardenangelist Books

Published by Gardenangelist Books

Indianapolis, Indiana

Editor: Deb Wiley
Managing Editor: Katie Elzer-Peters
Copy Editor: Billie Brownell
Designer: Nathan Bauer

ISBN-10: 0-9986979-5-8
ISBN-13: 978-0-9986979-5-6

Printed in the United States of America

To my nieces and nephews,
from your favorite gardening aunt.

CHAPTER 1

HAPPY NEW YEAR, GARDENERS

The first day of January isn't the beginning of my gardening season. Yet when the clock strikes midnight on New Year's Eve, I still end up with a long list of resolutions geared toward improving my gardening life.

If I resolve to lose weight and get in better shape, it is so that when I go out to mow the lawn for the first time in the spring, I can mow both the front and back lawns without stopping to take a nap halfway through.

If I resolve to read more, I start with a big stack of gardening books.

If I resolve to eat better, I grab a seed catalog to find out what I can grow that will help me improve my diet.

I have a standard list of actual gardening resolutions I bring out every year. They are like those plants we try to grow over and over. Even though we know we aren't likely to keep those plants alive for long, we seem compelled to try to grow them again anyway. I try to succeed with these gardening resolutions even though I know I might fail before the spring thaw.

Every year, I resolve that I will not buy any more

plants unless I know exactly where I will put them in my garden. This resolution usually lasts until the first trip to the garden center in the spring. But lately, with so many options to buy plants online, I sometimes overachieve in breaking this resolution, smashing it by late January.

I also resolve that I will immediately plant every plant I buy and not allow a plastic pot jungle to languish all summer on my back patio. Then every fall, I rush around before the first snowfall to shut down that year's jungle by putting every plant in its forever home. It would be shameful for a new jungle to spring up so quickly. But then it happens. By Memorial Day, the Garden of Waiting in Plastic Pots is taking up half of the patio. Plants are languishing in their hot, plastic pots with their branches leaning toward the garden, wondering when they'll get planted.

I look out over the frosted weeds in the garden in January and immediately resolve to weed more often and more regularly so that the weeds don't take over the garden again. When snow covers my garden in the middle of winter, this is an easy resolution to make and keep for at least six weeks if not two months. What an achievement! Then the garden begins to thaw out and right on cue, never missing a moment of opportunity, the early spring weeds sprout up and take advantage of the first warm rays of sunshine. When I see the number of weeds and notice how vigorous they are, I sigh and change my annual weeding resolution to "I'll try."

I'm so good with gardening resolutions that I even resolve to accept responsibility myself and not blame the garden fairies for every little thing that seems amiss in the garden. I resolve to accept responsibility for lost tools and missing left-handed gardening gloves. *Of course* I will accept responsibility. Later, when I realize it is convenient to blame the garden fairies when yet another gardening knife goes missing, I drop this resolution from the list.

My best gardening resolution is my promise to myself that every time I step out into my garden, I will pause at least once to enjoy the entire garden before the sun sets. Now that's a resolution I think I can keep.

CHAPTER 2

THE JOY OF GARDENING IN YOUR SECOND HALF-CENTURY

The passage of time. No one escapes it and no one should mind facing it—compared to the alternative. Yet there is nothing like the major holidays at the end of the year and a looming winter birthday to remind me that time flies and the passage of time is affecting my gardening. Once I hit 50 years old, I started to think about gardening differently than I did in my younger days.

After age 50, the point-and-tell-the-man-where-to-dig method seemed like a better way to dig holes than the digging-the-holes-yourself technique. Of course, the ideal situation is to have a lovely garden by the time you turn 50 so it doesn't require a lot of digging to keep it going. Since that isn't always the case, asking for help is a brilliant idea. The same holds true if you have to spread a lot of mulch or dig up a yard of sod. Point and tell the man where to dig. Save yourself for the important task of dragging a chair around to various parts of the garden to figure out the best spot, perhaps in dappled shade, for sitting and viewing the garden.

By the age of 50, I had spent so much time with my hands in the dirt that before I shook hands with someone, I automatically clapped my palms together to knock the dirt off, and then in one swift, stealthlike maneuver, I wiped my hands across my backside to make sure the dirt was really off them. I'm sure no one noticed. This is the universal gardener's handshake: clap, clap, clap, wipe, and extend a hand to shake. I'll admit if this handshake becomes a habit it can be a little embarrassing to do it someplace like in church, unless you went straight from the garden to church or have been helping in the church garden.

Around age 50, I realized the best time to plant trees was 20, 30, or more years ago. Then I would have had a good chance of enjoying them when both of us, me and the trees, were in our prime. The other best time to plant a tree, at least around my temperate garden, is in the fall. If fall planting isn't possible, then planting in the spring is acceptable. The main thing is to plant a tree wherever you have a good spot for one. Don't dither around about doing it because waiting one or two or more years will only lessen your future enjoyment of the tree.

What else did I learn as a gardener by the time I turned 50? I figured out all the best methods of medicating myself for aches and pains after a day in the garden. We all have our favorites. I also learned, though, that keeping myself in good shape is as good a medicine as any, along with drinking lots of water and asking or begging someone else to do the heavy lifting and digging.

I more fully appreciated a few ingenious inventions when I hit 50. I got excited about having a good magnifying glass, one I can hang from a cord around my neck to keep it within easy reach to read the fine print on seed packets or see the details of tiny flowers and insects. I also figured out how much I love a kneeling pad with handles to help me get back up. Whoever invented that kneeling pad is a genius—or likely a genius gardener over the age of 50.

When you turn 50 and you've been gardening for a long time, you are also more likely to find some old seeds lying around, remnants from past growing seasons. It's worth testing those seeds for viability because I have also figured out in my advanced years that money doesn't actually grow on trees. If those seeds are still good they are worth money. They are worth planting.

After age 50 I also learned that as much as the world has changed, not a lot changes in a garden. We still dig holes to plant, we still sow seeds, and we still enjoy our time in the garden, even more so than when we were younger. We praise the garden for keeping us fit, both in body and in mind.

The world, too, knows gardening helps keep a person young. Have you noticed the abundance of photographs in advertisements for retired people showing them in a garden, with a trowel in one hand, some pretty flowers in the other hand, and bright smiles on their faces? They've learned what we all learned. The best of life is enjoyed in a garden.

CHAPTER 3

ONCE UPON A GARDEN

Once upon a garden, there was a gardener who loved most kinds of plants. Actually, she loved all kinds of plants. She bought plants that she liked and plants that she loved. She let plants follow her home to her garden and even kidnapped some plants she had no business taking. Once she got the plants home, she found places to plant all of them in her garden, for the most part. Some of the plants were long-time favorites. Others were plants that happened to catch her eye at the garden center.

Sometimes she would look at her garden, point at a bare spot and announce, "I need a shrub here." Then off she would go to the garden center to look for a shrub. Though limited by what the garden centers sold, she would eventually find a shrub, or three or five shrubs, bring them home, and plant them in those bare spots. She did the same with trees and perennials.

Soon she had lots of shrubs and trees and perennials in her garden. For the most part, she was living happily in her garden, enjoying all she had planted.

Then one day, she looked at her garden and decided that something was missing. There were plenty of plants,

plants that she loved amid plants she had settled for, plants that she didn't particularly like, and plants that she had gotten from others. There were plants everywhere.

She couldn't help but notice all the plants together lacked a certain cohesiveness, a sense of place. She thought a lot about this. She studied her garden and looked at her plants and realized her garden was planted all higgly-piggly, without much thought about the overall design. This made her sad because she didn't think she had a good eye for design.

She knew others had a good eye for design so one day, she sent an email to a garden designer and explained her dilemma. She wrote about how she loved plants and gardening but needed some help. She wrote about the size of her garden and how one-third of it would be devoted to growing vegetables. She wrote that, though she knew a lot about plants, she didn't know much about garden design.

The garden designer responded to the email and came to see the gardener's garden on an early spring evening. She patiently listened as the gardener went around her garden talking about all of her plants and all of the flaws of her garden. The gardener told the garden designer all her hopes and dreams for her garden. Later the garden designer returned on her own to the garden. She looked at it and walked through it and studied it and took pictures of it.

Then a few weeks later, the garden designer returned with a garden design and went through it with the gardener, explaining it and describing it. The gardener looked at the design and studied it and asked some questions. She asked for a few tiny changes and then waited for the garden designer to come back to tell her how much money it would cost to replant her garden to follow the design.

Good garden design isn't free, my friends, nor are plants or mulch or strong workers who can dig and transplant and tote and carry to turn a gardener's collection of plants into a well-designed garden. You can, of course, spend a lot of money without a good garden design, but the result might be like pairing plaid pants with a striped shirt. Both are loved, both may fit, but they don't belong together.

It didn't take long for the gardener to decide what to do next, and so she said, "Yes, let's do this; let's turn this collection of plants, this haphazard design, into a new garden, one with a design that will showcase all the plants."

And she gardened happily ever after.

CHAPTER 4

DEAR LOUISE SHELTON

Dear Louise,

You do not know me but I know a little bit about you. I know you wrote a book in 1906 called *The Seasons in a Flower Garden: A Handbook of Information and Instructions for the Amateur.* I also know you gardened and lived in New Hampshire.

I know you once had a little spaniel named Idol, who for 12 years was your shadow in your garden, because you dedicated your book to him.

About your book, Louise. I suspect you had good intentions in writing it. Who would write a book about gardening with other than good intentions? I enjoyed your book and moved along pretty well through most of it, especially admiring the photos, so unusual for a book so old.

I was especially intrigued by what you described as an ideal garden with its rather formal look. I kept in mind, of course, that when you wrote your book this strict adherence to a specific layout may indeed have been an ideal garden.

Louise, should I ever decide to uproot my own garden and turn it into a Victorian-style garden, your book will be one of the first books I'll consult.

However, if I may offer a word of advice for your book, you should consider removing chapter XXV titled "Don'ts" from future editions. To put it bluntly, this list of 46 items, all starting with the word "don't," could cause even the most experienced gardener to wither in the garden. It could leave her standing there, rooted in place, wondering what she could do that wouldn't violate one of your rules. For example:

> Don't let manure come in contact with bulbs and roots.
> Don't fail to water plants in the dry season.
> Don't fail to stake and tie plants that require it.
> Don't plant roots in a doubled-up position.
> Don't pick flowers without scissors.
> Don't …

If I may be so bold as to point it out—your list of don'ts seems so *stifling*, like a hot, humid summer day, like a corset pulled too tight around your waist.

I know you meant well with your chapter of don'ts. You could even argue that each admonition of what we shouldn't do is a useful piece of information. I fear, though, that an inexperienced gardener could misconstrue your intent and try to follow each one of your statements exactly. The result would be a Garden of Don'ts, which is likely to fail and could even turn a budding gardener away from gardening right from the start. I know you would not want that, Louise.

I have no other complaints about your book and find it to have been an enchanting Victorian rabbit hole to wander through. As I wrote in the beginning of this letter, I believe your intentions were good as are the intentions of anyone who writes a gardening book of any kind.

Best wishes to you and Idol.

Hortifully,
Carol

CHAPTER 5

HERE COMES THE MULCHMOBILE

A quick inspection of my car provides even more evidence that I'm a gardener. If I were to get a new car, I would immediately figure out how many bags of mulch fit in the trunk and how best to arrange the bags to fit the maximum number for each trip. I would calculate this for different-sized bags. The forty-pound bags of topsoil, the two-cubic-foot bags of mulch, and even the three-cubic-foot bags of mulch. Bags of sand? Well, that's some serious math so it's anyone's guess.

I would also swear on a stack of seed catalogs and promise myself that I will never put bags of mulch or topsoil in the back seat of a new car. Later I will change this vow to I won't put bags of mulch in the back seat of a car without covering the upholstery with plastic first.

The same is true of plants. I once bought something called a trunk tidy from a company in England to hold the plants upright in the trunk. Leave it to the gardening British to come up with such a practical item. I also keep a trowel, some plastic bags, and an extra pair of gardening gloves in my trunk tidy so that if someone offers to let me dig up a little plant, I'm ready. I'm sure I've surprised more than one person with how quickly I was able to rustle up those supplies before they even finished making their generous plant offer. I have spare pruners, too, in case they offer a cutting of some rare-in-cultivation botanical prize.

If the plants I buy are too tall to fit in the trunk, I put the trunk tidy in the back seat and pack the plants in like passengers. I know if I can visualize all the plants in the car, I can eventually fit all the plants in the car, even if it means using the front passenger seat for some of the plants or using the lap of a person who wants a ride home in that front passenger seat.

Years ago, I decided enough was enough and bought a truck for gardening. This opened up a whole new world of possibilities. I could buy big tractor scoops of mulch and topsoil. Tall trees, short trees. Flats and flats of flowers. Garden sculptures and furniture that would never have fit in a car. One of my neighbors remarked that it was exciting to watch to see what I brought back in my truck each time I took it out for some fresh air and garden shopping. My truck, named Christo after the famous English gardener Christopher Lloyd, is my accomplice, the Ethel to my Lucy, encouraging me to push the limits on what might be prudently hauled home to my garden.

And my car? Well, my current car is a white SUV named Vita after Vita Sackville-West who famously had an all-white garden at her estate in England. Now

Christo, the truck, and Vita, the SUV, sit side by side in the garage, arguing over who gets to drive for the next garden shopping adventure.

CHAPTER 6

AIRING OUR DIRTY LAUNDRY

I would love to see a commercial for a laundry detergent that features a gardener coming in with dirty clothes, instead of some kids who've soiled their jeans by playing baseball or football or rolling around in the mud. These kids are amateurs when it comes to dirty clothes. Look at a gardener's jeans after a day of weeding, digging, mulching— what we call "gardening." Those are professionally dirty clothes.

During the gardening season, I often divide my laundry up into loads of lights, darks, and gardening before I wash anything. It has been a good week if the fullest laundry basket is the one marked "gardening."

I don't worry too much about how well a laundry detergent works on my gardening clothes. Grass and mud stains on the knees of my jeans are badges of horticultural honor and not dreadful stains that must be removed. Unless I've worn my good jeans to garden in, again. Then it would be nice to get the grass stains out. Otherwise, it doesn't matter much. After all, my gardening jeans will be stained again within five minutes of wearing them in the garden the next time.

The same is true of the white socks I wear out in the garden. After one day of gardening, they look like an abstract painting with streaks of brown from mud and green from grass against a dull white background.

I garden best in my faded green T-shirts, the well seasoned ones that have lasted for years. One T-shirt had a little hole on a shoulder seam. Out of the corner of my eye, that little hole looked so much like a bug that I found myself swatting at it every 15 minutes or so when I forgot, yet again, that it was a just little hole in my shirt and not a bug. I finally retired that T-shirt with a proper ceremony and then wrote it a letter expressing my gratitude for its many years of service through sweat and soil.

I have also attempted to do laundry while gardening, running inside to throw some clothes in the washer, then running back out to the garden. I liked to consider it efficient multi-tasking. Let the washer and dryer work while I garden. Then I would run back in to pull the freshly washed clothes out of the washer and throw them into the dryer. This sometimes resulted in freshly washed, non-gardening clothes with muddy handprints on them. I had no idea how dirty my hands could get in the garden until I came in and touched clean clothes.

In the interest of coming completely clean about my laundry, I confess I have found some unusual items after washing some gardening clothes. Plant labels come out especially clean after washing, with the writing still legible. It makes me wonder why the writing fades so quickly on a label out in the garden if washing it in a washing machine set to maximum agitation doesn't fade it. Seed packets, on the other hand, wash as well as most paper does and end up as goopy messes to wipe off the inside of the washer. And I know from experience that pruners make a *clunk-clunk-clunk* noise if they are washed in a washer and then tossed in the dryer.

Someday, with all my experience with dirty gardening jeans, grubby socks, and sweat-soaked T-shirts, I should be in a laundry detergent commercial. If I am, I'd love it to be a retro commercial. I'd pull a clean towel out of a box of Breeze detergent, and Dolly Parton would poke her head in the window and tell me how nice my clothes, and my garden, look.

CHAPTER 7

GAMES GARDENERS PLAY

I started playing the online game Words with Friends several years ago. It's like Scrabble® without the trademark infringement. My user name contains the word "gardener" in it, as anyone who knows me would expect.

Words with Friends helps me remember gardening words. When an opponent plays a gardening word I think they are stealing my words. Then I remember that I can still play that same word someplace else if I have the right letters. I can hardly wait to get the letters Z, O, Y S, I, and A so I can play the word "zoysia" and get lots of points, maybe across a triple word space with the Z landing on a triple letter space. Deep down, though, I think that if I ever did get those letters, I would likely get the message, "Sorry, 'zoysia' is not an acceptable word." That would squelch my dream of scoring lots of points with a gardening word. I hope I never have to find out if it is a valid word or not.

I have also played a lower scoring word because it was a gardening word. Yes, even though the word "hoe" is only worth five points, unless you land on some of the doubling and tripling spaces, I've played it because, well, it's my word. I guess the inner thrill of playing words that are garden-y overrules any desire I have to actually win a game. When I get letters like H-F-S-E-D-O-J in my tray, I hope there is a place to play the word "hoes" on the board, never mind that "joes" is a valid word and would be worth many more points.

My garden-related game playing doesn't begin and end with Words with Friends. I have a whole stack of board games that relate to gardening, including a garden edition of Scrabble®, a game called The Garden Game, and the garden edition of Monopoly® called Garden-Opoly. Garden-Opoly looks the most interesting. Instead of going to jail, you go to weeding. Gosh, does no one like weeding?

I can't truly say how fun these other games are. My friends refuse to play them with me, assuming that with my extra gardening experience, I'd beat the gardening pants off of them. I argue that's not true because they don't wear gardening pants.

Sometimes it is the luck of the dice roll, the draw of the letters that determines who wins a game, just like in the garden, where a little luck in the weather department and a few good plant choices can make a difference on whether you have a good tomato year or have to sneak in and out of the farmers market to buy your tomatoes. Regardless of your success, you're playing the game, you're gardening, and that's really all that matters.

CHAPTER 8

GOING STEADY IN THE SPRING WITH PANSIES AND VIOLAS

Every spring, I renew my love affair with pansies and violas. They are universal flowers! No matter where you garden, there is a season or two for growing pansies and violas. In my garden, I plant pansies and violas both in early spring and early fall. They are like bookends to keep the beginning and end of a growing season upright with summer in between.

I used to cruise around all the garden centers and big-box stores in early spring looking for pansies and violas so I could buy the first ones put out for sale. I'd peer behind the fences of the big-box store garden centers to see if they were still using their outdoor patios as extra storerooms or if they had cleared out enough room to set up a little table of pansies and violas.

Eventually I was able to stop cruising when I found a local grower who always had pansies and violas for sale early in the spring. No more driving around from one big-box store to another, hoping to score some flowers! I'm going steady with my grower now so I don't need those other places. My grower has strict instructions to call or email me or send me a message on Facebook as soon as the first pansies and violas are ready to sell. She knows she shouldn't sell them to anyone else until I've come by and purchased the ones I want. That's what good growers do when you go steady with them.

Sometimes I think it would save time and money to overwinter potted up pansies and violas so the same ones blooming in the fall are blooming again in the spring. Maybe it would be nice if I could get them to survive the heat of summer with a fresh blush of bloom once cooler weather arrived.

Then I realize I don't want my spring pansies to look like my fall pansies. In the fall, I want my pansies and violas to be brooding, mysterious, and fall-like in shades of dark purple, magenta, orange, and golden yellow. They should match Halloween decorations and mix in with the browns of the Thanksgiving garden.

In the spring, I want my pansies to be dancing and happy and jumping for joy in the pastel colors of Easter, including white, pink, violet, and purple, with a soft buttery yellow for accent and a bright yellow for pop.

Fortunately, Mother Nature takes matters into her own hands to resolve my pansy and viola seasonal color conflict conundrum for me. Even if I try to keep fall pansies and violas growing through the winter, by spring the scraggly survivors are ready—even begging—to be taken to the compost pile.

Fine by me! That empties the containers for a fresh bunch of spring pansies and violas. Because it isn't those actual flowers I'm going steady with, it's the grower, and we've got a date for early spring.

CHAPTER 9

FIVE PLACES TO HIDE YOUR PLANT PURCHASES

Spring is the season for gardeners everywhere to flock back to their local garden centers and greenhouses and load up on new plants for their gardens. My local greenhouse is packed with all kinds of pansies, violas, and other frost-tolerant flowers in the early spring, begging me to buy them and take them home. Buy I will, to the tune of many flats of flowers. I'll return several times as the season warms up to buy up summer annuals, perennials, and even some shrubs and trees.

I do realize there are some people—let's call them non-gardeners—who think one flat of mixed flowers is a huge plant purchase and all the plants they will need until the next spring.

Never mind them.

Once I take my plants home, I like to plant them as soon as possible so there is no evidence of the number of plants I purchased. I don't want to give anyone a reason to point to a patio full of plastic pots and flats of plants and ask, "You bought all these flowers?" or, "Are you starting your own garden center here?"

However, I understand there are times when we can't

plant out all of our plants as soon as we get them home. The plants end up sitting around in their flats and plastic pots waiting for us to have the time to plant them out or find the space to plant them in. Knowing that some non-gardeners will look at the quantity of flats and pots that accumulate after a rousing, fun-filled day of garden center and greenhouse hopping and question why we need so many plants, I am offering some valuable advice on places to hide your plant purchases.

Do you have foundation plantings around your house? I know one gardener who puts her newly purchased plants behind her foundation shrub plantings. This helps to protect the plants from the wind and sun while she decides where to plant them. It also makes them less noticeable to anyone who happens by, like her husband. On occasion, she has even found plants she hid that she forgot she purchased. What joy there was in finding them later! It recaptured that warm feeling she had when she first bought them.

An alternative to putting the plants behind shrubs is to place them in empty spots in a perennial border. If you use this method of hiding plants, be sure to keep them watered. Potted plants can dry out quickly in full sun.

How about decoy containers? If you have any large empty containers not yet planted, you can put several pots of newly purchased plants in a large container to hold them until you are ready to place them out in the garden. If anyone happens to see them just explain you are getting to know them better before planting them.

Note that if you have large plants still in their plastic nursery pots, as a last resort to make them look less like plants you bought and never planted out, you can spray-paint the pots and call them decorative container plantings.

Did you know some neighbors have perfectly good open spots on their patios and beside their houses where you could temporarily hide a few plants? The perfect situation is if you and your neighbor are both gardeners. You can keep one anothers' plants until you are ready to plant. Then if someone asks if you bought all those plants you can truthfully say you didn't. They belong to a neighbor.

You can also hide your plant purchases by planting them as soon as you buy them. This takes careful planning and a bit of time but is the best hiding place of all. Later, if someone asks if there are a lot of new plants in the garden, you can point at an old plant and say, "That plant? It's been here for years." If they point at a new plant, never confess it is new. Instead say, "This plant? Doesn't it look great there?"

And a bonus place to hide your plant purchases is to bravely leave them out in the open in their flats and plastic pots. Someone will ask, "Did you buy all those?" Your answer, of course, is to stand up straight and tall, wave your trowel at them like a sword fighter ready to strike, and say, "Yes, I did!" and leave it at that.

CHAPTER 10

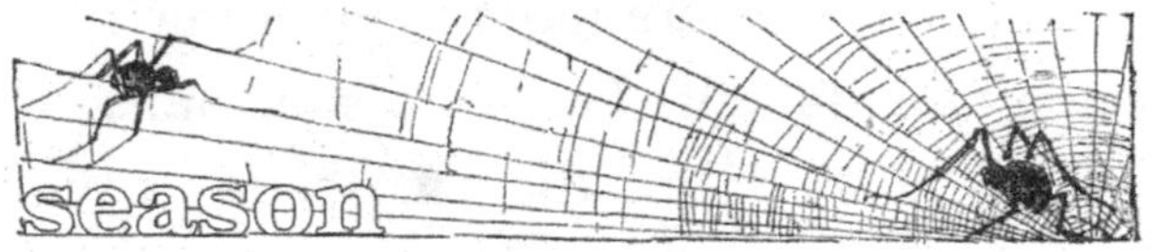

THE TALE OF PINKY AND PRETTY

By Pretty the Tulip

Everyone thinks the life of a tulip is quite simple. We get planted in the fall, hunker down all winter, then come up and bloom in the spring and soak up the sun juice to rejuvenate our bulbs. Then we rest all summer, fall, and winter, and repeat the process the next spring.

If only that were true. There is much more to the life of a tulip, as Pinky and I will tell you, because one of the worst things that can happen to a tulip happened to me and Pinky this spring.

We were almost smothered by weeds.

I'll tell you the tale. Pinky and I came up early in the spring, on schedule, sending up our foliage first, and then our flower buds. At first, all seemed quite normal. Sure, there were a few cold mornings that had us shivering in our roots, but we are used to that so didn't mind at all. Then one day, Pinky turned to me and said, "It's getting crowded around here."

I looked around and Pinky was right. It was crowded.

There were weeds all around us. There was a large family of purple deadnettle and a dandelion, too, encroaching on our space.

We didn't know where those weeds came from but they teased us and taunted us. They stole our food, the nitrogen in the soil. They tried to shade us out. The dandelion even grew a big, long taproot and kept trying to crowd out our bulbs where no one could see it, like a kid who pulls your hair when the teacher isn't looking.

They were thugs. It was awful.

Pinky and I didn't know what to do. We tried to shout for help, but couldn't shout loud enough to be heard, even with "tu lips."

Then Pinky suggested we should bloom as big and bright as we could and hope for the best. I agreed. We gave it our all and bloomed like we've never bloomed before, Pinky and I. Finally, after what seemed like days, a gardener came by and saw our blooms among the purple deadnettle family and the dandelion.

Fortunately for us, the gardener was carrying some weeding tools with her and immediately set about freeing us from the clutches of the weeds.

I don't mind saying that both Pinky and I were quite brave through it all, even though that sharp weeding knife came close to us a few times. We've heard of weeding tragedies that involved innocent flowers like Pinky and I being deflowered before their time. It's frightening to see that blade so close to your tender parts, too, as Pinky can attest.

Thankfully, the gardener was careful. She talked to us in a soothing voice through the whole rescue. "There, there, lovely little tulips, I'll get rid of these big ugly weeds. They won't bother you when I'm done with them."

Then, weed by weed, she freed Pinky and me from their evil clutches.

To show our gratitude to the gardener for rescuing us from the clutches of those weeds, we are going to bloom this spring for as long as we can.

And we vow to all that we will come up every year and bloom in gratitude as long as we can and never forget the gardener who rescued us on that lovely spring day.

CHAPTER 11

ON THE GOOD SHIP *RAIN AGAIN*

Springtime

Dear Leslie,

Greetings from the good ship *Rain Again*. We've had quite the journey through spring so far. We've sailed along with six or more inches of rain in the last ten days, depending on which rain gauge you believe. My garden is thoroughly saturated from it all.

The cruise director on the good ship *Rain Again* has kept me busy while we've been out to sea. I've been using the time between the ports Partly Sunny and Partly Cloudy to read and write.

I'm not complaining about how long we've been out to sea, though, because I was once dry docked, like you were, and felt quite abandoned in a hellish place called Record Setting Drought where we gardeners had little we could do except wring our hands, gnash our teeth, and pray for rain. After that once-in-a-lifetime experience, I won't ever whine again about sailing on the good ship *Rain Again*. I'd far rather be out to sea on *Rain Again* than docked at Record Setting Drought any day of the week.

Yesterday we dropped anchor at Frosty Morning, which was quite a surprise to those passengers who had already planted their tomatoes and peppers. We seasoned travelers know better than to plant this early in May. The winds can shift after a few warm days and then the captain seems to reverse course too sharply. The result is he runs right into Frosty Morning.

Fortunately we didn't stay long in Frosty Morning or go there later in May. Though, there was that one spring. Was it '97 or '98? That year the captain pulled a fast one on us, and we docked at Frosty Morning on May 25. Even *I* didn't see that port of call coming and lost all my peppers and tomatoes to the frost and had to replant.

Anyway, looks like we've docked at Partly Sunny now so I'm going to go up to the main deck of this good ship *Rain Again* to check the skies. If it looks clear out to the west, I'll get off at this port and stay as long as I can.

Safe travels to you as you sail on your own ship through the choppy waters of spring, or in your case stay docked at Will It Ever Rain Again.

Your Friend Always,
Carol

P.S. We've docked several times at Go Ahead, Buy Some Plants, so I've got a lot of plants to get into the ground before we set sail again on the *Rain Again*, which could be as early as tomorrow morning.

CHAPTER 12

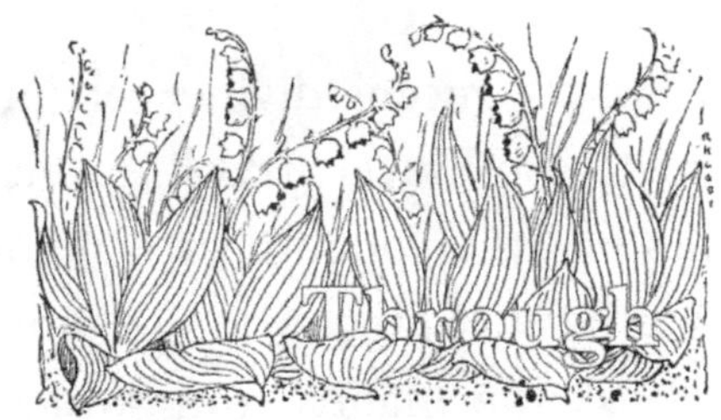

LEARN TO LOVE YOUR INSECTS

Gardening is much more enjoyable if you aren't afraid of insects. After all, a garden is full of insects. On any given fall day, swarms of bees, wasps, butterflies, and moths are sharing the pollen and nectar of asters, goldenrod, tall sedum, and other later-blooming flowers in my garden. They don't mind me, and I don't mind them as we each go about our business in the garden.

On the roses, I often find a creepy looking praying mantis doing some acrobatics in an effort to avoid me. This strange looking creature causes many people to shiver and run the other direction when they see one. Not me, though. I like to stop and watch and remind myself that once I, too, would have jumped away at the sight of a praying mantis.

Then I learned more about insects.

Now only a few creepy crawlers around my garden cause me to run the other direction, but not the praying mantis. It's an especially interesting and good insect to have in your garden. From the pages of an old book, *Insect Friends and Foes* by William Atherton DuPuy (The

John C. Winston Co., 1925), I learned a bit of folklore about them.

"Its name, mantis, means diviner, or fortune-teller. The English call it a soothsayer and old-fashioned people over there believe that its long finger will point the way home to a lost child. In France young women go to the crossroads and ask the mantis from which way their lovers will come."

The praying mantis is also fascinating for its real purpose in the garden, which is to eat other insects that are more harmful to the garden than it will ever be. That's why it is considered a beneficial insect that should be left alone when it's found. In the fall, it is not only eating bad bugs, it is also laying eggs that will overwinter and hatch in the spring as nymphs. These nymphs will eat aphids and other harmful insects. Now, who's going to run away from a praying mantis knowing its folklore and how good it is for the garden? Let it be. It's a friend to gardens and gardeners everywhere and to lost children and young women, at least in England and France.

The same is true of other insects, not that they provide directions or tell the future, but they serve some useful purpose in the garden, even if they are eating the leaves of the cabbage or sucking the juice from a rose.

I leave them be and let Mother Nature decide who lives and who dies, who goes and who stays. Generally, that method works pretty well for me. It worked especially well for my dad one summer when he brought in some composted cow manure from a nearby farmer. He took us kids with him, and we helped shovel the manure into large trash bags to bring back home and add to the vegetable garden. That summer, he grew some of the biggest tomato and pepper plants we had ever seen. His zinnias were six feet tall and the leaves of his zucchini plants were large enough to shade an entire village of garden fairies under one leaf.

But hidden in that manure was a life we didn't see. That summer, the entire back yard was overtaken by millipedes. Whatever good nutrition came in that composted cow manure must have been accompanied by millions of millipede eggs that all hatched that summer in our backyard. For most of the summer, we couldn't walk across the patio without stepping on a millipede, nor could we sit on any bench or chair in the garden without brushing a few of them off. We were horrified, but we never resorted to bug sprays. Somehow, Mother Nature figured out what to do and the next summer, we saw fewer millipedes.

There are some bugs we don't want in our gardens, like the infamous Japanese beetles that William Atherton DuPuy tells us arrived in the United States via one nursery in New Jersey around 1916. Who could have imagined what the next 100 years would be like as one gardener after another discovered those wretched, rose-eating, plant-eating devils in their gardens? Those beetles are a long way from home with no natural enemies. What's a gardener to do? Try a little hand-to-hand combat? Yes, with one hand you can pick the beetles off the roses and toss them in a bucket of soapy water held in the other hand. They will drown and die.

Hopefully, insect invaders like Japanese beetles are the exception, not the norm, so most of the time, we can love the insects in our gardens. Let Mother Nature figure out who eats who and which ones will survive the cold winter or the dry summer. Then we can marvel at their beauty and live alongside the insects as they enjoy the garden as much as we do.

CHAPTER 13

GARAGE SALES AND GARDENERS

Whenever I host a garage sale in my garage, someone will look at the garden tools hanging together on long hooks in threes, fours, and fives and ask if any of them are for sale. I suppose they can't fathom someone owning that many hoes. And shovels. And trowels, rakes, and other assorted gardening implements I've acquired over the years. The simple answer is a polite "no," punctuated with a chuckle and a smile because how could *anyone* have that many gardening tools?

The real answer is that I refuse to sell any of my gardening tools at a garage sale for one simple reason. If I don't like the tool well enough to use it in my own garden, why would I foist it off on someone else? Maybe that someone else is a new gardener or a wannabe gardener. They might come to my garage sale and innocently pick up an old, useless trowel I decided to sell. *I* know why I'm selling the trowel. Perhaps it was cheaply made and isn't good enough for digging in anything but a sandbox. Maybe it is poorly shaped, or the handle keeps coming off. How could I sell such a tool? What if it caused the buyer to turn away from gardening because they didn't have a good trowel? My conscience just won't allow me to sell such tools.

I also don't sell any of my clay pots at garage sales. I'm convinced that the right craft idea is out there for me to someday make use of the stacks of various sizes of clay pots in my garage, even the broken ones. I am aware, too, that if I find the right craft idea, I may not actually follow through with it, but then again, I might. To this day, the pots all stay, as do all the old T-shirts, shorts, and jeans that I could decently wear in the garden. Once I'm done wearing them in the garden, no one else would want them anyway. Though I once read that the clothes we donate that no one else wants to wear are shredded and turned into a felted material used to line the insides of car doors. Imagine! We are all kept warm in our cars because of old worn out gardening, and other, clothes.

I have occasionally parted with canna rhizomes and dahlia tubers at garage sales. If you actually take the time to dig them up in the fall, you end up with way more than you can ever plant the following year. Those cannas and dahlias were popular items the years I sold them. I guess the fact that I grew them in my garden turned them into desirable passalong plants.

The real problem with garage sales for most gardeners is they often occur in the spring when it is difficult to give up time in the garden to gather, sort, price, and set up items for sale. Or they take place in the middle of the summer when it is too hot to think about spending much time outside in a garage. Or they take place in the early fall when, once again, it's hard to give up that gardening time.

The best solution for gardeners is to stockpile garage sale items in the wintertime and then convince a neighbor who doesn't garden—and there are far too many of them these days—to add them to their sale, whenever it is.

Then while you are cheerfully gardening and your neighbors are happily selling, you might end up with a stranger stopping by to ask you about a particular plant blooming in your garden. You will be happy to tell them all about it, happy to know that your time spent in the garden is worth way more than a morning selling or not selling your old gardening tools.

CHAPTER 14

A GARDENER'S GUIDE TO CLEANING A HOUSE

I am usually ready for a good session of cleaning up the garden. I look around for my best work gloves, my gardening hat, some sunscreen, and a few tools, and I'm ready to go, even if I'm going to someone else's garden to help them. However, suggest to me that it is time to clean up inside my house, and I will find all kinds of diversions, most of which have nothing to do with cleaning.

When my garden is at its peak in the middle of summer, I don't see the dust on the end tables in the house or the little bits of leaves and grass clippings that are swirling in the corner by the back door, causing indoor dust bunnies who reside there to scurry off to some other hiding place under a bed or a couch.

Outdoors, I wouldn't dream of mowing half the lawn and then quitting and leaving the mower sitting in the middle of the backyard for weeks on end. I don't have the same qualms indoors. In the house, I might start vacuuming on a rainy day not fit for gardening and stop to water a houseplant that is wilting. Watering can lead to dusting the plant or taking it to a sink to give it a good cleaning. Maybe I'll decide to repot the plant. Off to the store I go for a new pot and some potting soil. That's how momentarily stopping housecleaning becomes more than a pause of a few minutes. It can be hours, days, or even weeks before I get back to cleaning. During all that time, the vacuum cleaner sits right where I left it.

I'm just following the advice of the late, great comedienne Phyllis Diller who advised housewives to leave their vacuum cleaners out all of the time. Then if unexpected company stopped by and your house was a mess, you could casually wave your hand in the general direction of the sweeper and tell them how you were just getting ready to clean the house. No one needed to know otherwise.

Regardless of your cleaning methods—or rather your methods to avoid cleaning in favor of gardening—we all know that a house isn't going to be as clean when the gardening season is in full swing. As you go out to the garden and back in to the house, dirt will sneak in with you, and once inside, it unfortunately doesn't leave on its own accord like you do on a sunny day meant for gardening.

Personally, I like to do a good inside cleaning before Easter and hope that holds the house until at least Thanksgiving.

If during my hiatus from cleaning during the warmer months those leaves and grass clippings pile up too high in the entryway, I can grab a broom and sweep them out to the garden. Once they are out in the garden, I am compelled to clean them up because I want the garden to look nice. It's a mind game. If I need to mop the floor because it is so sticky it holds me in place when I want to run out to the garden, I water the houseplants. Then I grab a mop and clean up any water I spilled on the floor. That's gardening, not cleaning!

CHAPTER 15

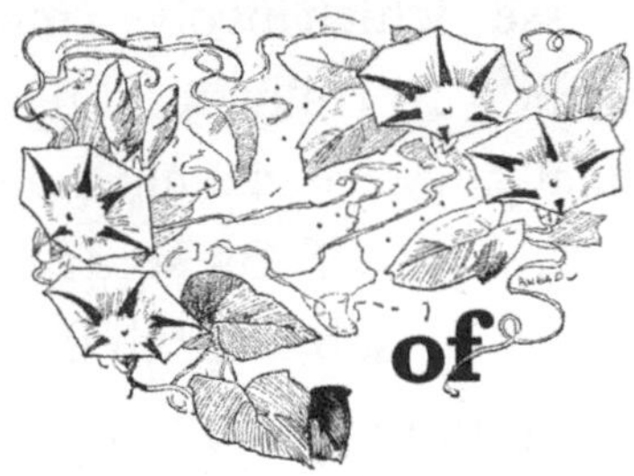

CLUB HORT

Normally, my houseplants stay in the sunroom and never leave except during some summers when I decide to send them to Club Hort, an exclusive all-inclusive resort where they will enjoy the finest of amenities.

Upon arrival at Club Hort, which is on the patio not too far from the sunroom they live in most of the year, my houseplants receive an updated wardrobe in the form of a topdressing of the best potting mix money can buy. It's labeled "professional" so I know it is the best.

Following that, they receive a shower of the purest water from the outdoor spigot to remove the dust, grime, and dander they've accumulated after months, if not years, spent indoors.

Then on a regular basis, they dine on a fine diet of organic nitrogen, phosphorus, and potassium mixed with occasional micronutrients. On some days, they drink the wettest rainwater the sky can deliver to them. I'm sure they enjoy the rain, but I hope it doesn't spoil them as they will only get city tap water once they return home to my sunroom.

Throughout their stay at Club Hort, they are enrolled in daily exercise classes, which involve a movement called "swaying in the wind." To really build up their strength they also occasionally engage in a more aerobic exercise called "blowing in the wind." On some days, often late in the afternoon, they are subjected to the most rigorous exercise, surviving a thunderstorm with strong winds and frightening flashes of lightning.

Their luxurious accommodations are in the shade, with glimpses of dappled sunlight, to ensure they don't get any leaf burn. Each morning, the local birds awaken them with sweet whistling and soft cooing. Each evening they enjoy after dinner entertainment provided by the fireflies performing a light show choreographed to the songs of crickets chirping. Then they are lulled to sleep by the soft sounds of water splashing playfully from the sides of a nearby fountain.

Prior to their return from Club Hort, each plant receives a thorough cleaning, which includes a vigorous scrubbing of the inside and outside of their pot. Once again, their roots are encased in the finest potting mix money can buy before they return home to the sunroom.

Some of the plants can be apprehensive about their vacation at Club Hort. They have been in the sunroom for so long they've forgotten what it is like to be outside. A few of them are even afraid of having to share their pots with spiders, bugs, and the like who may take up residence with them. I'm sympathetic, but I still make them go to Club Hort for their own benefit.

Once the houseplants get over the exhaustion of

traveling from the sunroom to the great outdoors of Club Hort, the change of scenery, the fresh air, the better light, the exercise, the regular watering and feeding do them quite a bit of good. When they return home to the sunroom, well before the first frost, they are bigger, stronger, and overall healthier because of their stay at Club Hort.

CHAPTER 16

TOMATO GROWING LESSONS FROM MY DAD

Are you a staker or a cager?

I'm a staker because my dad was a staker, so I assume his brothers and sister were also stakers, along with my grandparents, though I don't know for sure.

We had a neighbor who was a cager, but otherwise seemed to have a pretty good vegetable garden.

Of course, I am referring to the two primary methods of supporting tomatoes: staking and caging. Some of us do it properly by staking the tomato plants; others just throw some kind of cage around the plant and hope for the best. Not that there is anything really wrong with caging your tomato plants, but I was raised to stake tomato plants.

Some of the other lessons my dad taught me about growing tomatoes:

- Plant tomatoes deep in the ground after the last frost, removing all but the top two or three sets of leaves, and burying everything below those leaves in the soil. Roots will grow along the buried stem, giving you a sturdier plant in the long run.
- Enrich the soil around the tomatoes with your best compost. The tomato is the queen of the garden. It deserves the best soil in the garden and the sunniest spot in the garden. The tomatoes will be the biggest plants, so plant the rest of the garden around them. When I plan my own vegetable garden, I figure out where to plant the tomatoes first, and then everything else falls into place around them.
- Start early if you want to harvest tomatoes before anyone else. You have to start your seedlings six to eight weeks before your area's last frost-free date, pot them up a few times in progressively bigger pots, and then be willing to take the tomato plants out on warm days and back in on cool days and cold nights until it is finally time to plant them out in the garden. My dad did this, which is one of the reasons he always seemed to harvest his first tomato in June, and why I don't harvest a tomato until at least the middle of July, or later. At least I know *what* to do to get an earlier tomato, even if I don't do it.
- Provide sturdy stakes for support, expecting the tomato plants to get really big. My dad used metal fence posts, sunk nearly two feet down into the

ground with metal cross bars between them, to support his tomato plants. Believe me, his tomatoes needed such a sturdy structure. His tomato plants, in my mind, grew over eight feet tall. If you use puny stakes, expect a puny tomato plant. As the plant grows, tie it to the stake to keep it from flopping over.

- Remove the suckers from the tomato plants by pinching them off. This keeps the plants from getting bushy and expending energy on side shoots instead of blooms. Suckers, for those new to tomato growing, are the side shoots that form in the axils between the leaves and the main stem. Pinching is easy to do, if you keep up with it.

If you follow my dad's tomato growing advice, by mid-summer you'll have healthy, tall tomato plants with lots of delicious, juicy, homegrown tomatoes. And you'll be honoring him, one of the greatest tomato growing gardeners I've ever had the privilege of learning from.

CHAPTER 17

AN EXPLOSION OF ZUCCHINI

When the Independence Day holiday rolls around on July 4, in addition to celebrating the actual holiday I pause to take stock of my vegetable garden. On this day, I measure my corn plants, which I have been told since I was knee high to my dad should be knee high by the Fourth of July. I wondered, though, whose knees should we use to measure? Now I realize it doesn't matter whether it is a bee's knees, a kid's knees or a father's knees because the corn is always nearly shoulder high by early July.

By the Fourth of July, I should have also planted out all the annual flowers and picked at least one or more zucchini squash. If I haven't, I am officially behind in the growing season. I wonder if our founding fathers thought about the timing of this when they signed the Declaration of Independence? Did they anticipate it would become a gardening holiday, one we would use to determine if we were ahead or behind in our vegetable gardens?

In early July, I search my cookbooks for recipes to make use of my annual explosion of zucchini, wondering why I again planted so much of it. When I look at the piles of squash on my kitchen counter in high summer, a recipe calling for one cup of squash seems like a waste of time. I need recipes that call for four or even five cups of squash. Otherwise my meals for the foreseeable future will consist of all things zucchini including grilled zucchini, marinated zucchini, baked zucchini, zucchini bread, zucchini muffins, zucchini casserole, and my favorite, zucchini pie.

I know all about the old tricks people threatened to do to get rid of their abundance of zucchini. Tricks like leaving it on the neighbors' doorsteps, ringing their doorbells, and then running away so they don't know who has blessed them with free food. Would they guess it is the only person in the neighborhood with a vegetable garden? We hear about gardeners going to the local swimming pool or shopping mall and leaving zucchini in any car left unlocked. That seems much more anonymous. Of course, I never used any of those tricks. I prefer to look the receiver of my fine gift of squash in the eye, daring them to refuse it.

Another secret way to get rid of extra zucchini squash is to not pick it. After a while the plants will get the message and stop producing new fruit as they struggle with their oversized squash. Then in the nick of time, before the plant gives up entirely, you can saunter by, exclaim about the big squash you never saw, pick it, and bury it in your compost pile. You may feel guilty about doing this. After all, squash is food, and wasting food is wrong. But big squash is beyond being food for anything other than worms. You can compost it without guilt and proceed to enjoy the Fourth of July as intended—with lots of food made from zucchini squash and a side or two of sweet corn.

CHAPTER 18

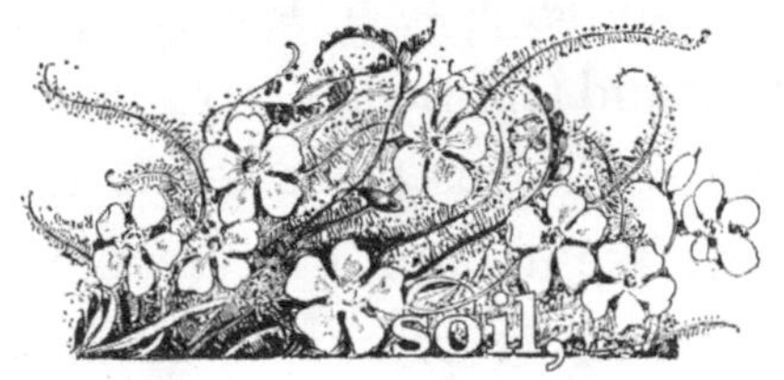

A LETTER FROM SUMMER CAMP

Mid-July at Camp Garden-A-Lot

Dear Mom and Dad,

Our camp counselor told us that we should write home from Camp Garden-A-Lot, so that is what I am doing.

I'm not sure how you chose this place, but you should know that we have taken to calling it other names such as Camp Not-Weeded-Much on account of the weeds all over the place. Some of the campers like to call it Camp Moles-In-Control because it seems like all summer there has been a mole running around here, and no one seems to be able to trap it.

Finally, I took matters into my own hands and put some poisoned worms in one of the active mole runs and reset a trap there, too. At least I think it is an active run. We'll see. If I end up killing the mole by either trapping it or poisoning it, I bet I get to be the Camp Garden-A-Lot Camper of the Week.

Of course, Camper of the Week doesn't mean much except I get some kind of trophy. I just hope it isn't the dead mole stuffed and mounted on a board. By the way, if you know of another way to kill that mole off dead, please write back and tell me.

Sometimes we call this place Camp Raining-Again because it seems like it rains a lot here. The other day it rained all day, and we campers had to stay indoors. You would have thought we would have done something useful with our time, like sort plant labels or make something with all the zucchini squash we picked, but mostly we sat around, looked out the window, and read our gardening books.

Speaking of squash, we sure do eat good at Camp Garden-A-Lot, as long as we are willing to pick our food. Tomatoes, green beans, cucumbers, squash, onions, kale, eggplant, Swiss chard. It's all there for us to pick and eat to our stomach's content. Oh, and peppers. They grow lots of both hot and mild peppers here at the camp.

Pretty soon, we also expect there will be a few ears of corn to pick. The counselors promised we would do something special when the corn was ready to pick. I hope by special they don't mean watch the raccoons eat it. We did that one year, and it is not nearly as fun as eating the sweet corn ourselves.

Our counselor said that tomorrow is going to be hot, so we campers are getting up early, about sunrise, so we can pick green beans and weed before it gets too warm. Yes, I will be sure to put on extra sunscreen.

What else is going on at this gardening camp? Well, not much, truthfully.

At night we like to watch the fireflies lighting up the

garden. They say if you look directly at a firefly's light, just past it you will see a garden fairy. I've been trying it every night but haven't seen a garden fairy yet. I did, however, feel a tickle on my toe after I went to bed. I hope that was a garden fairy and not a spider. You know I don't like spiders, especially when they are in the bed with me.

Oh, I almost forgot. I have special responsibilities to fill the bird feeders here and let me tell you, I have to fill them every day, especially the peanut feeder. If I don't, those big ol' bluejays give me the stink eye until I do. Trust me, you don't want to get on the wrong side of bluejays.

It sounds like I don't like Camp Garden-A-Lot, but honestly, I do like it and plan to return every summer for as long as I can. I like it even when the only recreational activity is mowing the lawn. Mowing sure is fun even when it is hot out. Which reminds me. Can you send me a new string trimmer? The one here keeps jamming and not letting out new string, so I had to stop trimming. I just mow now. But it would be nicer if I could also trim, and it might get me another Camper of the Week award if I did.

Your Loving Daughter,
Carol

CHAPTER 19

TRAVEL TIPS FOR GARDENERS

I read once that traveling around the country in an RV for the summer is not a good lifestyle for a gardener. The thought of leaving their garden during the height of the growing season? No self-respecting, card-carrying gardener would ever think to do that. If they did, they would have to leave a long list of instructions with a garden caregiver.

When I travel, I plan my vacation destination based on the gardens I want to see. When we used to have phone books, I would flip through the yellow pages as soon as I had checked into a hotel to see what garden centers were in the area. Now I look online well before my trip to see what gardens and garden centers are in the area so visits to them are included in advance in my itinerary.

After a few days of visiting one or two garden centers and gardens on vacation, my hotel room begins to look like a conservatory, with plant purchases lined up on the windowsill. Some people ask for lower floors upon checking in, or rooms near the emergency exits or away from the elevators. Not me. I ask for south-facing windows to ensure my plants get good sunlight before they start their journey home.

I realize that some of the plants I've purchased while on vacation are also available from my local garden center. I am quite aware of that as I lovingly pick them out and figure out how to get them home. Why do I do this? Because purchasing plants from places that are a long distance from my own garden gives them a nice story. It makes them a souvenir, one that is much better than a plastic back scratcher or nail clippers engraved with the name of the city I visited.

For gardeners, traveling by car is preferred over flying. It allows us to bring back more plants. If forced to fly, gardeners have come up with many creative ways to bring plants home, including bare-rooting them, wrapping them in plastic, and putting them in checked-through luggage. If there isn't room for our clothes, we can always ship those home or donate them to a local charity.

The alternative is to carry the plants with us through the airport and on to the plane. The plants will be screened and we may get a few questions and sideways looks from other passengers, but any real or perceived embarrassment is worth it for the right plant.

When driving, we have to remember that passengers will still need room to sit in the car for the return trip home. They may not enjoy riding for hundreds of miles with a plant on their lap. Rest stops? Yes, plants need them, too, for water, fresh air, and a chance to get some real sunlight instead of light filtered through car windows.

The bonus of traveling by car, especially if we gardeners are the drivers, is it puts us in control of the route we take, which will coincidentally be past any public garden worth visiting as long as that garden is within a reasonable detour of our direct path to our vacation destination. But don't ask any non-gardening passenger what a reasonable detour is. They'll say a mile and every gardener knows it can be 10, 50, or even 100 miles.

One other bonus of travel away from your own garden, beyond the ideas you get from seeing other gardens in other climates, is how sweet your garden will look to you upon your return. It will have grown and changed in your absence so you'll get to see and appreciate it all over again. You'll remember upon seeing it that there is no place like home, especially when home is your own garden.

CHAPTER 20

READING THE NEWSPAPER

The tradition of stepping outside to grab the morning paper and then scurrying back in before neighbors see you in your pajamas or robe is quickly going away. Who gets a newspaper delivered these days when you can read the news online as soon as it happens? For gardeners, if they still do get an actual paper, a trip outside to pick it up is fraught with peril and distraction, especially if it involves actually walking down the driveway to the mailbox to retrieve it.

On my walk down the driveway to get the newspaper I might see a weed that needs to be pulled and decide, right then, that after weeks of ignoring that weed, I've given it enough of a head start. Now, while I'm still wearing my pajamas, is the time to pull it out. Of course, it won't come out of the ground with a simple tug. Why should it? I've given it weeks to establish itself with deep roots. So with my newspaper tucked under my arm, I walk up to the garage to get a weeding tool, laying the paper down so I can I grab the tool and a bucket to put the weed in.

Then with my weeding tool and bucket in hand, I head back and realize the weed has friends. Lots of friends. I begin to weed, forgetting that I'm still wearing my pajamas and am in full view of the neighborhood. One weed leads to another weed. Then I decide some flowering plants would look better if I removed their spent blooms. I head back to the garage to get the pruners and then go back and remove those tired blooms.

My bucket is now full of weeds and spent blooms so I step around to the side gate to go around to the back garden and dump the contents onto the compost pile. Looking down at my feet, I realize I am still wearing slippers, which are now wet from the dew on the grass. Oh well, they can't get wetter than wet so I head on back to the compost pile. After dumping the weeds and clippings, I go back into the house through the back door, take off my wet slippers, and slip on the closest shoes at hand, which happen to be gardening shoes.

Now I'm in my house, wearing gardening shoes, wondering where I left the newspaper.

When I finally find the newspaper, it's still folded in half, revealing a frightening headline: "Top Mercury-Emitting Plants." A little shiver runs up my spine as I glance toward my garden. I had no idea plants emitted mercury. I wonder if any such plants are growing in my garden. How is it even possible for plants to emit mercury? I recall the elements I once learned were needed by plants. Mercury was not one of them. All these thoughts only take a few seconds before I turn the newspaper over and see the rest of the story.

Power plants. They weren't referring to garden plants at all. They were writing about huge, mercury-belching factories of energy. I was safe, or at least safe from my garden exposing me to mercury.

Now, if I can just stop exposing my neighbors to the sight of me gardening in my pajamas …

CHAPTER 21

IS YOUR NEIGHBOR AN ECCENTRIC GARDENER?

I have the qualifications and experience to provide a list of clues to determine if you have an eccentric gardener living next door to you. It isn't necessary to know how I can provide such a list. Just go through the list, and answer yes or no about each of your neighbors. As you go through the list, you should also see if any of these clues apply to you. If so, you may be that eccentric gardener the other neighbors are talking about.

The clues, in no particular order:

- She has a pair of gardening clogs at every entrance to her house and garage. At a moment's notice, she can slip on a pair of gardening clogs and be outside in her garden, chasing a rabbit or scaring a squirrel away from her recently germinated green beans.
- You occasionally see her lying on her stomach in her lawn. But when you see her lying on her stomach in the grass, you don't panic and call for help. You wait a minute or two, and sure enough she soon gets up. She was merely taking a picture of

the garden she thought should be taken at ground level.

- She often spends afternoons in the fall sitting on the lawn, jabbing it repeatedly with a long, narrow trowel as she plants another couple hundred bulbs for spring flowers.
- You are never earlier than she is no matter how early you get to the local greenhouse to buy spring violas and pansies. By the time you think to buy spring flowers, she's already purchased her flowers, planted them up, and given them individual names. You swear the owners of the greenhouse must call her to let her know when the flowers are ready for purchase. As it turns out, they do.
- When you see how many gardening tools and hoes she has hanging in her garage, you wonder if she has set up a shop to sell them from home. You also wonder why she has more than one lawn mower.
- When UPS brings her packages, nine times out of ten they are marked "Live Plants." The tenth package looks suspiciously like the shape of a hoe.
- She has a truck decorated with bumper stickers with sayings like *Practice Random Acts of Gardening* and *#GARDENING*.

If this is your neighbor, don't panic. She is harmless and is most likely fascinating to watch as she putters about her garden sowing mysterious seeds, planting bulbs, and growing more plants than you ever thought possible. Accept the fact she is the neighborhood's eccentric gardener and say "thank you" when she hands you a basket of her fresh homegrown tomatoes on a hot summer's day.

CHAPTER 22

ARE YOU YOUR NEIGHBORHOOD'S ECCENTRIC GARDENER?

Every time I step out into my garden, it teaches me a lesson, and one of the best lessons is to accept what is different from the rest of the world, at least as far as the world extends up and down my street. Different is the new black! Different is the new green! Different is the neighborhood's eccentric gardener!

Who cares if none of the other neighbors grow vegetables? If you want to plant a big ol' vegetable garden and grow enough tomatoes for yourself and the entire block, by all means do it. You may be different, but you will eat well all summer.

Who cares if the neighbors all have plain porches and stoops with nary a spring blossom to be seen after the snow melts? If you want to plant two long boxes and four pots of violas and pansies on your porch as a salute to spring, you should. Plant some flowers in a window box, too. Then later you can switch out those pansies and violas with the heat-tolerant petunias and geraniums of summer. You may be different, the neighbors may be staring, but you will be smiling every time you step out onto your front porch.

Who cares if you were the only one kneeling in your lawn with your broad backside in plain view of anyone who walked by that fall day you planted bulbs out front? Your neighbors might plant a token dozen or so bulbs in the fall while you plant bulbs in multiples of a hundred for the best show. You may be different, but you'll have the earliest blooms and the most blooms in the neighborhood every spring.

No, it doesn't matter that the neighbors weren't even aware of the contest for the earliest bloom. You are different. *You* were aware. You've won!

Don't be afraid to garden, to choose the plants you love, even if they aren't from the palette of ten plants—or is it five?—that all the neighbors grow. Beautyberry with purple berries? You bet! Pawpaw trees in the back garden? Yes, naturally. And a quince tree, too. You are different. You are the neighborhood's eccentric gardener. Good for you.

Don't be afraid to invite garden fairies into your garden to share early blooms with the pillywiggins. Chase after lightning bugs in the summertime. Lie down in the lawn and watch the bees in the clover. Make a necklace out of those clover flowers and then show the neighborhood kids how to make them, too. Jump in a pile of leaves in the fall. You'll enjoy the difference it makes in the joy you get from your garden.

Don't be afraid to different. Live the lessons of the flowers. Be your own gardener. Be the neighborhood's eccentric gardener.

CHAPTER 23

GUIDE TO CERTIFIED GARDEN FAIRY HABITATS

The question on many gardeners' minds is how to determine if they have a certified garden fairy habitat.

Before you can even ask if your garden is a certified garden fairy habitat, you need to go through the following checklist and make sure you can answer yes to each one.

- Do you have a garden and is it free of pesticides? If yes, it may be garden fairy certified. If no, then why are you even bothering to answer these questions?
- Do you have flowers in your garden? Flowers are required for a certified garden fairy habitat. The more types of flowers you have, the better the garden fairies like it. They need a variety of flowers including those with petals, like daisies, that they sew together for simple, modest garments. They also need bell-shaped flowers for their hats. And they like to see flowers blooming year-round.
- Does your garden attract birds? Wherever there are birds, there are garden fairies. If your garden attracts a good number of birds—beyond nasty

ol' starlings—then chances are good you have a garden fairy habitat.

- Does your garden have a water feature or other source of clean water? Even a birdbath can help ensure a garden is suitable for garden fairies.
- Does your garden include edible plants, such as vegetables or herbs? Many gardeners don't plant vegetables, which is sad because garden fairies love vegetables, especially tomatoes, green beans, and lettuce. If you have no vegetables but have some plants with edible fruits you may still have a certified garden fairy habitat because fortunately, garden fairies also like edible fruit. If you have nothing edible in your garden, what do you expect the garden fairies to eat?
- Are there good hiding places in your garden? If you can't decide if there are good hiding places, lay flat on your stomach in the middle of the garden and look around. Do you see hiding places? Surely you must! Where do the birds go when the neighbor's cat slinks in? Wherever the birds hide, there you are likely to find a garden fairy or two or three or even a dozen.
- Do you laugh in your garden? Laughter attracts garden fairies. Yelling does not.
- Is there dappled shade in your garden? Garden fairies do not like to sit out in the blazing hot sun so you must have some shade for them.
- Is your garden a little bit messy? Garden fairies abhor perfection in a garden. They much prefer

a few weeds and some flowers that should be deadheaded. But the garden can't be untended. Garden fairies will not stay long in an untended garden.

- Do you spend time in your garden? If you do, you may find that your pruners, trowels, and gloves go missing when you are out working in your garden. Why? Because one of the garden fairies' favorite ways to pass the time is to hide tools and watch gardeners look for them. It's a laugh a minute for them, even while it is frustrating for the gardeners. In fact, the more frustrated the gardener gets while trying to look for lost tools, the more fun the fairies have.

If you answered yes to all of the above questions, congratulations! Your garden qualifies for consideration to become a certified garden fairy habitat. Unfortunately, if you answered no to even one of the questions, you probably don't have a garden fairy habitat of any kind, certified or not.

If you answered yes to all the questions and know you have a possible garden fairy habitat, how do you know if it is certified? Only the garden fairies themselves can certify a garden fairy habitat, but chances are, they will in due time if all your answers are yes.

If, to my great regret, you don't believe in such creatures as garden fairies, you should still follow the guidelines above in your garden. It will ensure it is a garden anyone would be proud and happy to be in because what makes a garden good for garden fairies makes it good for gardeners, too, even if they don't believe.

CHAPTER 24

THE MYSTERY OF WEED CONTROL

Every year seems like a marvelous year for weeds. I can't turn my back on a flower border or vegetable garden bed for more than two seconds before a new weed seed germinates. There are weeds everywhere in my garden.

Why? Apparently the mystery of weed control eludes me.

I clear out weeds in the morning and by nightfall they're back, and they've brought their weediest friends with them. The next day there will be a three-foot-tall weed in a spot where I looked the day before and saw no weeds. How did I not see such a prominent weed? The weeds hide like a zucchini squash hides itself under those big zucchini squash leaves and only show themselves when they are huge and menacing and ready for garden bed domination.

From thistles to dandelions to redbud seedlings, I have enough weeds in my garden at any given time to qualify for a world record. What's a gardener to do?

I long ago abandoned herbicides as too expensive and not worth the chemical exposure in my little garden.

I explored using so-called organic herbicides, including vinegar, and determined they are more hype than help. There is a reason they aren't labeled as herbicides, and that's because they really don't work that well as weed killers. Plus, they can be as harmful to the garden and the garden soil as chemical herbicides.

Sometimes I consider using boiling water to kill weeds, but on the scale I would need to use it, it seems impractical. To get to all the weeds, I'd be running back and forth with multiple teakettles of boiling water all day long and into the evening.

Many a hot afternoon I've sat inside and plotted and schemed and thought about how to vanquish weeds from my garden. Meanwhile, outside, the weeds don't mind the heat. They continue to grow. And flower. And seed. With long-lasting seeds. They spread their roots. Deep roots.

I wish I could just pull a few weeds and leave them lying around the garden to scare the other weeds. I'd love to stand and watch the scared weeds run for their lives, or at least cast their seeds outside my garden before they die. If only weeds could see other dead weeds and, thus terrified, run away.

I could toy with the weeds, and often do, by letting them grow right up to the point of flowering, before cutting them down or pulling them out. I know this may look like procrastination on my part, letting them grow like that when I know they are there, but I really do enjoy teasing the weeds, giving them hope, and then dashing that hope. I relish the idea of them becoming demoralized and giving up.

If only they *would* give up.

I could try the opposite approach. I could pamper the weeds and make them feel like they are the most prized plants in my garden. Then they would surely reward me by dying off. After all, it seems to me when we fuss over a plant too much, it usually dies from too much care. But I'm afraid that might backfire on me with the weeds because weeds don't behave like ordinary garden plants. They are stronger, faster growing, and more determined to take over than any plant I've ever bought for my garden.

What will I really do to control these weeds? I'll probably just keep pulling the weeds and whacking them back and get busy applying a good layer of mulch to the garden borders. If I do that, I'm bound to have some success with weed control, at least enough success so that my garden no longer qualifies for the world record.

CHAPTER 25

THE MYSTERY OF MISSING GARDENING TOOLS

What happens to those gloves, pruners, trowels, loppers, dandelion diggers, and other assorted gardening tools that disappear in the garden? One minute you are using a tool, and then you set it down, perhaps to pick up another garden tool or stop for a drink of water. When you reach to grab your tool again, it's gone.

You then stop what you are doing to hunt for it, feel for it, look high and low for it. It is nowhere to be seen. It was right there! You just used it. How could it be gone now?

But it is gone. As daylight turns to dusk, you finally give up your search, shrug your shoulders, and head in for the evening, still wondering where your garden tool is, pondering how you could have lost it right beside you, and hoping you will someday find it. There can only be one explanation as to what happens to these gardening tools.

Garden fairies.

The minute we turn our backs on our favorite

gardening tools, the garden fairies sneak in and snatch them away. They carry them off to the outer reaches of the garden in places we never knew existed: under shrubs and hedges, in that bit of brush near the fence line, perhaps even at the bottom of a compost bin. The more we love a tool, the higher the bounty for it, and the more likely a garden fairy is waiting for us to set it down so that, as quick as a puff of pollen can float up from a flower, they can grab it and run.

Then the garden fairies peer out from their favorite hiding places and watch as we wander the garden, looking high and low for that favorite tool, often looking several times in the same places, as if the tool is magically going to reappear. They know we won't find it in any reasonable amount of time. Sometimes, if we are lucky and have been good, the garden fairies will relent a little and return the tool to a spot where it will be in plain view. Then they howl with laughter and glee as we stumble across it and wonder how we missed seeing it in plain sight for so long.

The garden fairies play similar tricks with gardening gloves. A gardener takes a great risk when she pulls off her gardening gloves and shoves them in her back pocket. Maybe she wants to take pictures with her smartphone, which never works with gloves on. Or perhaps she is just going inside for a minute for a snack. Then when she reaches behind to pull her gloves out of her back pocket, there will only be one glove. Where is the other glove? There is only one answer. The other glove is with the garden fairies and may never be seen again.

Many gardeners do not believe in garden fairies. I suppose those gardeners believe in absent-minded gardeners, which is the other explanation for missing tools and gloves. That could be, or perhaps it is not so much that some gardeners are absent-minded as they are distracted. Distracted by what? A pretty flower? A butterfly floating by? The song of a bird they've never heard before?

Or distracted by garden fairies.

In any case, missing tools and gloves are a fact of gardening life. My advice? Buy two of each of your favorite tools, paint the handles bright colors, and never set them down, even in plain sight.

CHAPTER 26

RECIPE FOR AN ENCHANTING GARDEN

Ingredients

Early spring-flowering plants in a wide variety of shapes and sizes, including snowdrops and crocuses

Late spring-flowering plants, plus flowering trees and shrubs

Summer-flowering plants in a blend more interesting than just daylilies and daisies

Fall-flowering plants, especially purple flowers to contrast with fall leaf colors

Winter-flowering plants*

Clover, for the lawn

Vegetables, any you enjoy eating fresh

Interesting rocks

At least one lovely bench

An assortment of birdhouses and bird feeders

One water feature, as simple as a bird bath or as elaborate as a fountain or pond

At least one gardener

Optional: a pinch of tasteful garden ornaments

Directions

In a large area, prepare the garden beds by removing any grass and weeds. If you've chosen plants suitable for your area and climate, you should not need to amend the soil.

Plant all the flowers, trees, and shrubs around the garden to spread the blooms throughout.

Mix clover into the lawn to feed the rabbits and keep them out of the vegetable garden.

Plant vegetables in one area. If your neighborhood covenants don't allow vegetable gardens, put up a sign calling it an "Edible Source Garden" and plant flowers around the perimeter to hide the vegetable plants. Alternatively, plant edible plants throughout the rest of the garden.

Blend in the decorative elements, including interesting rocks, tasteful garden ornaments, a lovely bench, the birdhouses and bird feeders, and the water feature.

Visit the garden at least daily to pull weeds, deadhead flowers, fill bird feeders, and tend the vegetables.

Sit on the bench in the garden and watch as butterflies float from flower to flower, vying with bees for the sweet nectar. Listen to the songs of the birds. Eat any vegetables as they ripen and bring in fresh flowers to enjoy indoors.

Allow children to visit the garden, and anyone else who is interested.

When all these ingredients are in place, you will have an enchanting garden.

* Available from mail-order sources if not found locally

CHAPTER 27

THE LAST ACT BEGINS

The performers are getting tired and grouchy as they wait offstage for the last act to start. They're complaining to management that they haven't gotten enough water breaks, and it has been so hot they can hardly stand to be under the spotlights. But the garden show must go on to its finish. You, the gardener, are the playwright, director, stagehand, and audience of it all. You hope you've got enough in you and the garden for the final act to be as successful as the first act so many months earlier.

Finally, for the last act, the curtain rises on the first Monday of September—Labor Day—as a tiny yellow leaf breaks loose and falls from a tree, landing with a resounding thud heard by every single gardener. Gasp! Was that part of the script? Is this growing season really almost over?

There's a flurry of activity on the stage as the actors scramble to their marks, not quite ready for the curtain to go up for the closing act, but up it goes. The audience politely applauds. Will there be enough blooms in this last act before the final curtain—frost—falls on this year's garden performance?

Even while the asters bloom and the leaves turn colors, while the days grow shorter and the nights cooler, behind the scenes you're already setting up a new stage for the next gardening season. You look through the notes you've made on how to make the next show better than this one that is nearly over.

New trees. You recall fondly those early days when the trees seemed so small, like bit players. Now they are tall and wide and dominate scenes, in some cases, overpowering the other actors around them. Regardless of how well they act or don't act, they are hard to replace once they get so big. You decide, wisely, to rewrite some scenes for next year to take advantage of the larger trees.

New shrubs. The shrubs are often bit players taking part in a crowd scene. They may be asked to speak a few lines, perhaps with some blooms at key moments, but for the most part they tend to blend in, behave, and provide a good backdrop for any flowers you add, especially those with solos. Then you reconsider. Is it fair to the shrubs to relegate them only to bit parts? You make a note to give them a few more lines next year.

New flowers. You aren't sure this year's performance had enough color, enough pizzazz, enough bloom, so you decide backstage, where you are already working on props for next year's show, you will plant more spring-flowering bulbs for the opening scene of next year's garden show. You wonder if there were enough flowers performing solos that wowed the audience? If not, you make a note to put out a casting call for some new summer blooms.

Unfortunately, some weeds have rushed on stage and are planning a long, extended run through this last act. They are like a bad, drunken, vaudeville dance troupe, kicking their way around the garden, casting their seeds everywhere. It takes a big hook to get them off stage. You make a note to increase security—weeding—so next year they aren't allowed to recklessly spoil the entertainment.

At some point there will be a final curtain call—frost—and you will be left to clean up the theater. There will be leaves to rake, cast members to bundle up and send home, stage props to stow away for spring. Already, before the doors are closed and locked on this garden theater, you are making notes, writing a new script, and casting more plants—I mean players—for next spring's grand opening night.

Because you know what all gardeners know: the gardening show will go on, and spring—opening night—will be here sooner than you are ready for it.

CHAPTER 28

IF YOU DON'T LOVE YOUR GARDEN IN THE FALL

If you don't fall in love with your garden all over again in the fall, then perhaps you don't love your garden at all?

It's easy to love a garden in the springtime when every plant seems fresh and new. Every day there are new blooms, new leaves, new sprouts. And there you are, running from one springtime planting to the next—tired, dizzy, and euphoric as the growing season begins. It's all so wonderful and exciting, this fresh love you have for your garden.

It's easy to love a garden in the summertime. The days fall into a rhythm of sorts. After that sprint of spring, we need a steadier beat, don't we? We water, we deadhead, we pick tomatoes. We repeat. We lull ourselves into thinking the summer, the growing season, will never end. Then the first yellow leaf of a nearby tree falls gently to the ground and we begin to sense another change.

Fall is coming.

The garden starts to look a little shabbier. We see more seedheads than flowers. The vegetable garden is a shadow of its former glory. It seems pointless to keep watering plants that have few blooms left on them.

It isn't always easy to love a garden in the fall, but fall is when a gardener's true love for their garden shows.

Gardeners who love their gardens know that no matter how tired they are after the summer, fall is not the time to rest. They know there is too much to do in the garden in the fall for a gardener to relax and take it easy.

Gardeners who love their gardens in the fall plant bulbs, add a few more shrubs, maybe even plant a tree. They cut plants back. They rake leaves, always returning them in some form back to their gardens as mulch or compost. They straighten up borders, adding a few new planting areas in the fall. They know having those beds ready to plant before winter means spring will be a little less hectic.

Even as some plants die and other plants go dormant, in the fall those gardeners who love their gardens see life amongst the decaying leaves.

Gardeners learn they must love their gardens in the fall if they want to have a romance in the spring with their garden. They know fall, with its messiness of spent blooms, fallen leaves, and haggard weeds, is the season when we show true love for our gardens.

CHAPTER 29

MY DEAR FALL GARDEN

My Dear Fall Garden,

I must offer both thanks and apologies, along with new promises, in this letter to you, my dearest garden, for what you've been through these last few months and for how well you did, overall, in spite of what you went through.

First, I would like to get my apologies out of the way so we can end on a high note. I want to put regrets behind us and begin anew, if you will allow me.

I am sorry that the heat of the past summer drove me indoors and left you too often to fend for yourself with no rain and my occasional and rather lackluster watering to keep you going. I was not as faithful with watering as I should have been. There were even a few weeks when I let you go almost too far to recover. I truly am sorry.

Please know deep down—no doubt where you had to send roots to get water— I did care and always wanted to do better. Even when I left town for a week—all right, ten days but who's counting—I arranged for my sister to come and water. She did a great job, didn't she? The vegetable garden should be particularly thankful. I know she appreciated the tomatoes and squash it offered her for her hard work running around with hoses every evening.

We shall let bygones be bygones now, right? Surely you loved the rain that came in the fall, along with the cooler temperatures. I could see the weeds enjoyed the change in weather and how they flourished as a result.

Anyway, let us put all that heat and dry weather and my poor watering habits behind us and move on, together.

Now, for my thanks.

Thank you, my dear garden, for doing as well as you did through the hottest, driest summer you've ever experienced, that I've ever experienced, that anyone has ever experienced. You came through it marvelously and showed me what you are made of. You are made of tough plants and deep roots. You are made of flowers that wouldn't give up. My dear garden, you continue to show me every day how resilient you really are. Bless you. Thank you.

Now, my promise to you, my dear garden, is to fill you with more plants that do well when it is hot and dry. To love you each day with consistent watering and diligent weeding. To bring you new plants and flowers. To cover you with fresh mulch. To sit with you, enjoying our company together, no matter what the weather is. Through heat and drought, through cold and snow, through warmth and sunshine, I'm going to always be there for you. I promise. Truly, my dear garden, the best is yet to come.

I hope you know I am sincere. Didn't you see me out weeding the other day? And watering? Those two actions should prove to you how sincere I really am.

Not only am I sincere, I am also inspired anew, my dear garden, now that I see what a difference a little rain, a modicum of deadheading, and some weeding have made so far, in just a few days! I promise to return and continue the good start, the good restart, we've made together now that we've gotten some rain.

Thank you, my dear garden,

Hortifully,
Carol

CHAPTER 30

IT WAS A DARK AND STORMY NIGHT

It was a dark and stormy Halloween night. As I walked along a path in my back garden, dry leaves crunching under my feet, I thought I heard the sounds of someone else walking through the garden behind me. I stopped to listen, but I heard nothing.

Nearby an owl let out a screech.

I jumped at the unexpected cry of the owl and glanced quickly over my shoulder. I swear I saw something in the shadows, but I talked myself out of it. "There's no one here but me," I told myself.

Suddenly the wind stopped and all seemed calm. I stood for a minute in the stillness of the night and glanced up at the full moon just as a shadow crossed over it. I shivered and thought about turning back and running for the safety of the house.

I forced myself to continue down the path, still hearing the footsteps, which now seemed more like something hopping.

Hop, hop, hoppity hop.

I stopped.

It stopped.

I started walking again, this time a little faster. Then I

heard it again, and it seemed faster, too.

Hop, hop, hoppity hop!

I could feel my heart beating in my chest … *beat, beat, beat-ity, beat.* I wished I had brought a garden hoe with me, a hefty hoe, one that I could use to defend myself. I continued walking while glancing furtively back to see what or who might be in the garden with me. At that moment, a shadowy light came out of nowhere and brought it briefly into focus.

I gasped.

I may have screamed.

Horror of horrors, and nightmare of all nightmares!

My garden was visited by the gigantic …

Halloween Hare!

According to ancient gardening legend, the Halloween Hare hops from garden to garden on Halloween night looking for Easter candy not found in the spring Easter egg hunts. If that haunting hare doesn't find any candy, he will create a little havoc in the garden by pulling up plants or turning over containers. Many gardeners, hoping to avoid this mischief and mayhem, will leave a few pieces of old candy out in the garden for the Halloween Hare to find.

I've been told that sightings of the Halloween Hare are rare. I've even heard some gardeners don't believe he exists. I'm a believer now and will make sure to always leave a few pieces of old candy in my garden every year on Halloween night just in case that scary, haunting hare visits again.

CHAPTER 31

THANKSGIVING DAY DINNER CONVERSATION STARTERS FOR GARDENERS

For those of you who find yourself sitting at the Thanksgiving Day dinner table next to your second cousin's husband's mother or your niece's mother-in-law's daughter or some other person who is welcome but unknown to you until the minute you sat down, I have a few tips for keeping the conversation going in a gardening direction.

I would start by mentioning the mashed potatoes and sweet potatoes are not as closely related as their common potato name might suggest. Once you have their attention with this opening fact, you can continue to tell them about how sweet potatoes are tuberous roots from the plant *Ipomoea batatas* in the Convolvulaceae plant family while regular white potatoes are from the plant *Solanum tuberosum* in the Solanaceae family. For your grand finale on this topic, just as they are putting a big forkful of sweet potatoes in their mouth, announce that the morning glory is in the same family as the sweet potato. Ditto when they get ready to eat some mashed potatoes, only shout out "Petunias!"

Next I would talk about which table scraps are suitable for the compost bins and which are more suited to the trash can. Leftover sweet potatoes and their peelings can go in the compost bin but it would be best to trash the marshmallow topping. Who knows what those marshmallows are made of, and do you want them on your garden, even composted? The turkey bones, once they've been used to create a good turkey broth, also belong in the garbage.

I wouldn't tell them the story about how you once hosted a worm composter inside your house. Some people are touchy about discussing worms while they eat—as I've found out from past experience. Of course, if they are going after another helping of noodles, noodles that you want to eat, go ahead and talk about the worms to see if it ruins their appetite, leaving more noodles for you.

You might also talk about spring flower bulbs and find out who at dinner has planted some bulbs that fall. If no one has, fill them in on the many flower bulbs they can still plant if the ground isn't frozen.

What fun is Thanksgiving dinner without a little rant? The difference between Thanksgiving cactus and Christmas cactus (*Schlumbergera* genus) is a safe topic to argue about. You can lament about how these are already showing up in the stores in bloom, yet you haven't even snapped the wishbone of the Thanksgiving Day turkey.

Dazzle them with your knowledge that the Christmas cactus in the stores isn't the true Christmas cactus, but an imposter that is easier to grow and blooms earlier. This is another example of how everyone seems to be in a big hurry to get to Christmas as soon as Halloween is over. You can finish up this topic with a discussion about the differences between the two types of cactus—the Christmas cactus leaves are rounded while the Thanksgiving cactus leaves are pointed—and beg everyone to look for the true Christmas cactus wherever they shop. If they ever find a true Christmas cactus, tell them to buy several for you.

Finally, as you are sitting around the table staring at that last bite of pumpkin pie and wondering if you can choke it down, you should mention that yard work is a great way to burn off calories. If you aren't at your own house for Thanksgiving, don't press too hard on this topic, lest you be handed a rake and ushered outside by your hostess. Instead, tuck this idea away for the following day when you're at home and can use your own rakes as exercise equipment.

CHAPTER 32

TURNING BLACK FRIDAY INTO GARDEN FRIDAY

When Black Friday rolls around the day after Thanksgiving, I casually browse those ads that came with the local paper and start looking for the good deals on gardening tools.

I'm usually disappointed. Occasionally there might be a good deal on a gardening tool thrown in at the last minute at a hardware store, but finding them is like looking for a needle in a haystack of digital televisions, computers, video games, printers, and the new must-have toy of the season. I know from experience not to get my hopes up too high for great gardening bargains on Black Friday, unless I consider a computer a good gardening tool, which it is if you want to use it look up gardening information or read a few good gardening blogs.

But all is not lost. I save a lot of time not shopping on Black Friday. Instead I enjoy a Garden Friday tending houseplants indoors and going outdoors to spend time raking leaves, weather permitting. Plus, if I had the inclination to do so, I could place all those newspaper ads in the garden to smother weeds. They can become the bottom layers of a new garden bed or border. Or I can spread them out to protect the kitchen table that I've turned into a potting bench to pot up amaryllis bulbs for the upcoming holidays.

If I am foolhardy enough to face the crowds of Black Friday shoppers, I might go out to the big-box stores to see if they have any bins of flower bulbs left over, marked down to sell quickly before they throw them out. Then I think better of it and use the time at home to plant all the bulbs I've already purchased.

On Black Friday, I might get a text from one of my sisters asking me if it is too late to plant flower bulbs at the end of November. My answer is always the same. "You aren't shopping?" All kidding aside, my real answer is: As long as the ground isn't frozen, it isn't too late to plant bulbs. They will be okay, and they will bloom. What's the alternative? If you leave them in their bags in the garage they will definitely not bloom in the spring.

Some people have started to spend Black Friday doing the opposite of what retailers want us to do. Instead of fighting through the crowds, or hunching over the computer engaging in an online shopping spree, they spend time at home getting rid of the excess possessions we all have. Clothes we'll never wear, weird kitchen appliances we'll never use, books we'll never read. I do take umbrage, though, when friends suggest that some of my gardening books and gardening tools are excess and will never be used or read. "They spark joy," I tell them, or do whatever it is they are supposed to do for me.

Then I return to my Garden Friday, a day spent in the garden, or with my nose in a gardening book, away from the crowds, dreaming of next spring.

CHAPTER 33

FIVE YEAR-ROUND DAILY GARDENING HABITS

When the last summer-like days of October are past and the frost is on the pumpkin in November, it's time to get serious about preparing for winter and spring. As is my habit, I clear off the vegetable garden and leave it ready so I can plant peas and lettuce in mid-March without having to till up the ground. I make sure I have a stash of potting soil in the garage so when I buy the first pansies and violas in early spring, I will have what I need to plant a few containers to decorate the front porch before Easter.

Indoors, fall is the beginning of the gardening book and seed catalog season. All those gardening books and seed catalogs promise to entertain and enlighten me and give me hope through the winter. If they don't, well then, all hope is lost.

As I continue to work in my late fall garden, long after most of my neighbors have called it quits for the season, put up their holiday lights, and started their wintertime hibernation, I'm left alone to ponder what gardening is all about. I imagine ways to keep the gardening spirit alive when the air is frosty and there is snow on the ground.

It was during one of those quiet days when I came up with five daily gardening habits to keep in mind even when I cannot be in the garden.

- Smell a flower. Try to have some fresh flowers around you wherever you are. Sometimes the fresh flower is on a houseplant, and sometimes it is a stem or two of cut flowers picked up at the grocery store. Sometimes the flower doesn't even have a scent, but leaning in close to see if it does should put a smile on anyone's face.
- Touch a leaf. You can do this if you have a favorite houseplant nearby at all times. Be sure to keep the plant watered and give it some good light. If you want, you can also talk to it. Some say it helps the plant when you talk to it, others say it is foolishness. But there's nothing wrong with being foolish at times and maybe it does help the plant.
- Sow a few seeds. If you don't have any plant seeds to sow, and often we don't in the wintertime, sow seeds of kindness and helpfulness. Those kinds of seeds are free and can go a long way to add enjoyment to someone's day.
- Breathe some fresh air. If you can do that while gardening or exercising in a garden, so much the better.
- Get your hands dirty every day. Perhaps by

gardening a little outside. If you can't get your hands dirty by gardening, tend to your houseplants. Or get your hands dirty by cooking, or crafting, or doing something good that occupies your hands and mind and keeps you out of trouble.

CHAPTER 34

A LETTER TO MOTHER NATURE ABOUT WINTER TEASING

Dear Mother Nature,

I would like some winter, please and thank you. I love my winter. I don't want my winter to be like fall or spring.

Winter gives me the freedom to leave the garden for a little while and turn my attention to other activities like reading about gardening, napping and dreaming about gardening, and convincing myself it is too cold to be out in the garden doing any actual gardening.

However, sometimes temperatures in early winter hit record-breaking highs and occur on a weekend. When this happens, I feel guilty if I don't go out into the garden and do something. It is as though you, Mother Nature, are telling me, "Go outside right this minute, young lady, and cut back those perennials you didn't cut back earlier, and you do it before I send down the torrents of snow which will be your payback for these warmer than usual days."

After I hear that lecture, I go out into the garden and

start cutting back some perennials. Then I notice the egg case of a praying mantis so I stop because, Mother Nature, I was sure you didn't want me to destroy that, did you? Not to mention I'm not used to gardening outside in December, and it felt all wrong to be out there.

Mother Nature, what will be our payback for extra-warm winter days?

You know every person, whether they garden or not, is thinking we are going to pay for this warm weather come January and February. Can't have the good without the bad, right? What did we do to deserve this weather? What's the catch here? What's the trick? What's going to happen the rest of this winter, which has barely begun? We are going to have a blizzard, aren't we?! It's going to be awful! Where's the snow shovel?

By golly, Mother Nature, don't tease us like this. Don't leave us in suspense as to when you are really sending winter. We actually want some snow and winter because if it doesn't snow enough or get cold enough, we will soon be wringing our hands and muttering about the bugs and how many there will be next spring and summer and how big they will be if we, and by *we*, I mean *you*, Mother Nature, don't kill some of them off with the snow and cold.

But please don't provide too much snow and cold. After all, Mother Nature, I planted camellias and they are doing quite well so far with this warm weather. Did I also mention this is the best my Christmas rose, *Helleborus niger*, has ever looked, Mother Nature? Great job on those! Oh, and outstanding work on the Christmas coloring on the geranium foliage. Festive!

My kind request for the rest of this winter that is just beginning, Mother Nature, is to please send us some seasonal weather, and by that I mean a little snow when it is cold, and no precipitation on those days when you can't make up your mind on the temperature and it hovers around freezing.

No offense, but no one likes the ice. No one.

If you would do that, Mother Nature, I promise to make sure I cut back the rest of those perennials on the first warm spring day you send my way after Valentine's Day. You have my word.

With a shared love of gardening,
Carol

CHAPTER 35

HOE, HOE, HOE

We all know what Santa Claus wants for Christmas. He wants a hoe, hoe, hoe.

So does every gardener. Well, at least some of us would like a garden hoe for Christmas. I always consider the telling of that joke to be the official start of the Christmas season. Usually some new friend who doesn't realize I've heard that joke every year for decades, or at least since I claimed to have the world's largest hoe collection, tells it to me right around Thanksgiving. They were probably inspired by a crafter who was selling a wooden sign painted with "Ho, ho, ho."

The more clever crafters add an extra "e" on the end of each "ho" and fasten the sign to an old hoe. I know this because I have such a sign, a gift from someone who thought of me when they saw it and knew it would be a good addition to my hoe collection.

I now keep that hoe joke in my official collection of holiday hoe jokes, which fortunately includes only the one joke. But I have other Christmas gardening collections with more than one item. I've got rolls of wrapping paper, stacks of Christmas cards, and a tree full of ornaments that tie together gardening and Christmas. If a holiday item relates in any way to gardening, it has somehow made its way to my house where all things gardening are always welcome.

With four pairs of gardening shoes that look a lot like old Dutch shoes made of plastic, I'm always ready for the Dutch holiday tradition of setting your shoes out on Saint Nicholas Eve, December 5, in hopes that St. Nick will come by and fill them with candy. Though my gardening shoes are always by the door, I've never found any candy in them. Perhaps I didn't set them by the door with a fitting enough ceremony and high enough expectations? Maybe they were so dirty ol' St. Nick passed me by once again?

Part of my Christmas décor also includes a stack of gardening books related to Christmas, including *The Legend of the Christmas Rose* by Henry E. Jackson, published in 1914. I learned about the Christmas rose (*Helleborus niger*) several years ago and immediately planted one in my garden, followed by several more in later years. Sure enough, some years there are actual blooms on the Christmas roses around Christmastime—outdoors, in the winter, sometimes under snow—if one considers a fat, white bud a bloom. In the wintertime, I do.

I annually read a small book about Christmas plants that tells the story of the usual plants one would expect to read about. Poinsettia, holly, rosemary, cinnamon, and, my favorite, the evergreen tree. Sadly, there is no mention in the book of lily of the valley, which I found was often featured on vintage Christmas postcards, another collection that I started and soon narrowed down to "vintage Christmas postcards that feature plants and the occasional garden gnomes, elves, and fairies." Many of these vintage postcards feature lily of the valley as a holiday flower.

Now I have a new tradition of buying pre-chilled lily of the valley pips, which I pot up and force into bloom for the holidays. I haven't got the timing quite right on those flowers so they and I usually celebrate the holidays well into January when they finally bloom. What else does a gardener have to do in the wintertime?

If there is actual winter weather, a gardener hopes for mild weather, and a chance to relax in a warm spot by a sunny window and enjoy the blending of gardening traditions with Christmas traditions. Then before they can say "hoe, hoe, hoe," it will be time to open up the first seed catalogs.

CHAPTER 36

TWO RABBITS MEET AT THE END OF THE YEAR

At the end of the year, I imagine two rabbits meeting in my garden. Standing by the back gate is an old, tired rabbit reflecting back on his year in the garden. He ruminates about the weather, as do all gardeners, whether it was a good year soon to be forgotten for its normalcy or a bad year that will become legendary even before it is over. Those are the years gardeners talk about whenever they meet and swap stories. Do you remember the Drought of '12 and how dry it was? How about the blizzard of '78, which has thankfully never been equaled?

The old rabbit recalls fondly the new plants added to the garden during his year and the old plants that finally died under his watch or lack thereof. He remembers the abundant harvest of green beans offset by a poor year for peppers. He tucks away all these memories for safekeeping while waiting for a new rabbit to come along. He's tired, impatient, ready to go wherever old rabbits go when their year is over.

He goes through some notes of what he wants to

tell the next rabbit. He especially wants to tell him that the clover in the lawn is sweet and the gardener doesn't like it when he eats the green beans and lettuce in the vegetable garden. The gardener wants the new rabbit to keep up the myth she believes in, that all rabbits are cute and friendly and do no harm in her garden.

The new rabbit finally shows up as the clock strikes midnight. Hopping with boundless energy and new ideas, the new rabbit, who is a baby compared to the old rabbit, carries with him the two magic words that will revive even the most dejected gardener. It doesn't matter if the gardener has been through a drought or a flood, if they've had a crop failure or lost a treasured plant, these two words are the most hopeful words in all of gardening. They spur a gardener to action. They revive a summer-weary soul. They lift all gardening spirits. They give hope.

What are these two wonderful words? They are small words. With only four letters in each one. Eight letters in all, plus a space. They are powerful words. Magical. Invigorating. Inspiring. No matter how your growing season turned out, if you are a gardener, these two words will make you forget the disappointments, the heartaches, the body aches, the challenges of every sort that your garden threw your way. Whether your growing season was long or short, wet or dry, hot or cold, it doesn't matter.

With these two magic words, you'll forget the bad and remember the good. You'll be revived. You'll be champing at the bit to get into the garden again. You've no doubt said these two word many times, not knowing how powerful they were.

The two most hopeful words in all of gardening are:

NEXT YEAR!

Next year, you will have fewer weeds, bigger flowers, larger gardens, more vegetables.

Next year, the rain will come when you need it, the sun will shine on the weekends, and there will be no blistering heat.

Next year, there will be bees and butterflies on every flower but no aphids or leaf-eating beetles. The birds will sing louder from the trees.

Next year, you'll expand the garden, add new borders, clean up old beds, and have a garden you'll be proud to share with others.

Yes, definitely, next year all will be right in your garden.

Next year. Delivered to us every year by a young, energetic rabbit, eager for winter to end and spring to arrive so he, and we gardeners, can start a fresh gardening year all over again.

ACKNOWLEDGEMENTS

There were many friends and family members who spurred me on to write this second book of essays as a sister book to *Potted and Pruned: Living a Gardening Life.* This is the place where I tell you who they are and what wonderful things they did to help me with this book. But first, a story about why I love books you can hold in your hands, made with real paper and ink.

Somewhere on Earth, 2117

Lorac was one of the lucky ones. After the great internet crash of 2116, having access to books and the ability to read gave her a certain advantage over her peers.

Reading had been cut from the school curriculums 50 years earlier after it was determined most of the world's knowledge was available via videos. Why learn to read when you could just listen to knowledge? Writing, too, was deemed unnecessary.

Lorac was fortunate, however, because her great aunt, who had been taking care of her ever since her parents had joined a Mars expedition, insisted she learn to read, and not just read on a screen, but by holding books in her hands. She loved reading this way. There was something about the printed page that drew her in. Her great aunt had a library with countless books safely hidden away where no one could get to it without her permission.

Lorac could read books from her great aunt's library for hours and days and years and never run out of books.

Why did her great aunt have so many books? She had refused long ago to engage in the magic of tidying up or undertake Swedish death cleaning. She kept her books, and read them, too.

When the internet crashed in 2116 and all the videos were wiped out, the only knowledge left was hidden in books. Only those who could read had access to that knowledge.

Thus began a worldwide initiative to teach people how to read again. World leaders said their goal was not only to teach people how to read but also to teach them how to grow food since the world's food supply chain was broken during the great internet crash. Those who had gardens had more food than others.

Fortunately, Lorac's great aunt had hundreds of books on gardening and a little spot in her backyard to grow food.

One day Lorac was looking at all the books and playing a game she invented to choose which book to read next. She would close her eyes and run her finger across all the spines of the books on a shelf and then randomly stop. She promised herself that whatever book her finger landed on, that would be the book she read next.

It was her great fortune one winter day to have her finger land on a slim green book. She gently took it off the shelf, dusted off the cover, and noted the titled: *Homegrown and Handpicked: A Year in a Gardening Life.*

She began to read. She giggled a little. She laughed. She smiled. She fell in love with the idea of learning the long-lost art of gardening, of living a gardening life.

She showed the book to her great aunt, who nodded knowingly and with a smile said, "Yes, that is one of my favorite books. It was written by your great-great-great aunt who loved to garden. She was wise and knew her knowledge of gardening would last much longer if it was printed on paper and didn't just exist in an electronic format or as something told on a video. That's why she published her writings in actual printed books. You should definitely also read her first book, *Potted and Pruned: Living a Gardening Life*. I know it is around here somewhere."

Together Lorac and her great-aunt read these books cover to cover, recalling another saying hundreds of years older than even the books. "If you have a garden and a library, you have all that you need."

And with their ability to read, their library, and soon, a garden, they lived happily ever after.

I would like to thank Katie Elzer-Peters and her team at *thegardenofwords.com*, including Billie Brownell and Nathan Bauer, for their expertise in taking my manuscript and turning it into a beautiful book. I am indebted, again, to my content editor Deb Wiley, who provided countless suggestions and guidance chapter by chapter, and to Mary Ann Newcomer whose insight helped me further refine these essays. I would also like to thank my nephew, Ty Hayden, who turned "the mowing lady" I use as my Twitter avatar into a tiny logo for Gardenangelist Books.

Perhaps most of all, thank you to all those who read my first book, *Potted and Pruned: Living a Gardening Life*, for taking pictures of it in places as far away as India, England, Mexico, and throughout the United States and posting them on Facebook, for encouraging me with your positive responses and kind words. I hope you will all be as kind to *Homegrown and Handpicked: A Year in a Gardening Life*.

For those holding this book in your hands, there are words embedded in the graphics at the beginning of each chapter. These graphics originated from *The Garden's Story* by George H. Ellwanger (D. Appleton and Co., 1889). If you put all those words together in chapter order you'll discover my advice for how to live a happy gardening life.

If by chance you bought your copy of this book from me, you may also discover a note, an empty seed packet, or a bookmark slipped between the pages, reminiscent of some of the treasures I've found in old gardening books, placed there by previous owners long before I discovered them.

Thank you for purchasing this book and for taking the time to read it. I hope you find these essays enjoyable, especially if, like me, you strive to live a year round gardening life with humor and a sense of play and fun.

LOOKING FOR A LITTLE MORE INFORMATION?

I continue to post on my blog *maydreamsgardens.com* and encourage you to subscribe to it so you don't miss a single post.

Like many gardeners and authors, you can also find me on several social media outlets.

Currently I have two pages on Facebook:

- May Dreams Gardens, where I share about my gardening expoits.
- Gardenangelist, where I share gardening information I've found around the internet.

I am @Indygardener on Twitter, where I tweet about gardening and life, and on Instagram, where I mostly post pretty pictures of flowers and gardens.

If you are interested in getting involved with other garden writers, please check out GWA: The Association of Garden Communicators, *gardenwriters.org*.

If you think you would like to publish your own book, I recommend *thegardenofwords.com* as a place to start your search for assistance.

If you are interested in meeting other gardeners in your local area, join or start a garden club. Hang out at the local garden centers and greenhouses. Enroll in a Master Gardeners class offered by your local cooperative extension service. Start your own blog and tell the world about your garden. Just don't stay behind your garden gate, gardening alone.

And if you want to ask me something, feel free to email me at Indygardener@gmail.com.

ABOUT THE AUTHOR

Carol Michel is a lifelong gardener and resident of Indiana with a bachelor's degree in horticulture production and an associate degree in computer technology, both from Purdue University. She spent over three decades working in healthcare IT while making a life for herself in her garden. Now Carol calls herself a gardenangelist and spends most of her time in her garden, sharing all things gardening with anyone who will listen. She is an avid collector of old gardening books and claims to have the largest hoe collection in the world. Carol writes about her old books, hoes, and many other gardening-related topics for *Indiana Gardening* magazine and her award-winning garden blog, www.maydreamsgardens.com. She is also the author of *Potted and Pruned: Living a Gardening Life* (Gardenangelist Books, 2017)

CPSIA information can be obtained
at www.ICGtesting.com
Printed in the USA
BVHW07s1442180918
527791BV00008B/17/P